Truth Wins Jr. Media

The Newborn King

This book belongs to...

_____

...and I am a Child of God

If you are interested in other early education Bible activity books, adult word searches, prayer & devotional journals, and much more, scan the QR code to check out the **Truth Wins/Truth Wins Jr. Media** author page.

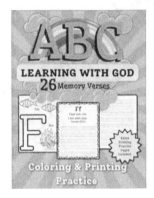

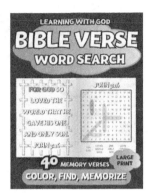

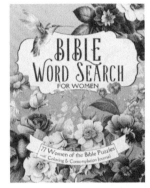
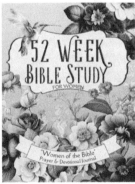

If you are pleased with this book, we would love your honest review. Just scan the QR code to get back to Amazon.com. Thank you!

Welcome to the world of **Truth Wins Jr. Media**! Our focus is to spread the Word of God while fostering opportunities for children to learn, have fun and grow their faith.

This book is intended to tell the story of the birth of Jesus. Starting with the foreshadowing of His birth in the Old Testament, the events leading up to His birth as well as the celebration of visitors following His birth.

May it be a tool for sharing the miraculous story of The Nativity. Color along with your little one, read them the verses, and celebrate the Newborn King.

What a wonderful way to learn about the true meaning of Christmas.

Train up a child in the way he should go;
even when he is old, he will not depart from it.
Proverbs 22:6

A Savior was promised...

"The days are coming," declares the Lord, "when I will raise up for David a righteous Branch, a King who will reign wisely."
Jeremiah 23:5

Therefore the Lord himself will give you a sign: The virgin will conceive and give birth to a son, and will call him Immanuel. Isaiah 7:14

And the promise was kept...

God sent the angel
Gabriel to
Nazareth, a town
in Galilee, to a
virgin pledged to
be married to a
man named
Joseph...
Luke 1:26-27

The virgin's name was Mary. The angel went to her and said, "Greetings, you who are highly favored! The Lord is with you." Luke 1:27-28

But the angel said to her, "Do not be afraid, Mary; you have found favor with God."
Luke 1:30

You will conceive and give birth to a son, and you are to call him Jesus.
Luke 1:31

In those days
Caesar Augustus
issued a decree
that a census
should be taken
of the entire
Roman world.
Luke 2:1

And because Joseph was a descendant of King David, he had to go to Bethlehem in Judea, David's ancient home. He traveled there from the village of Nazareth in Galilee.

Luke 2:4

He went there to register with Mary, who was pledged to be married to him and was expecting a child. Luke 2:5

While they were there, the time came for the baby to be born,
Luke 2:6

...she gave birth to her firstborn son and wrapped him in swaddling cloths and laid him in a manger, because there was no place for them in the inn. Luke 2:7

And in the same region there were shepherds out in the field, keeping watch over their flock by night. Luke 2:8

And an angel of
the Lord appeared
to them, and the
glory of the Lord
shone around
them, and they
were filled with
great fear.
Luke 2:9

And the angel said to them, "Fear not, for behold, I bring you good news of great joy that will be for all the people. Luke 2:10

For unto you is born this day in the city of David a Savior, who is Christ the Lord.
Luke 2:11

And this will be a sign for you: you will find a baby wrapped in swaddling cloths and lying in a manger.
Luke 2:12

And suddenly there was with the angel a multitude of the heavenly host praising God and saying:...

Luke 2:13-14

"Let's go to Bethlehem and see this thing that has happened, which the Lord has told us about."
Luke 2:15

So they hurried off and found Mary and Joseph, and the baby, who was lying in the manger. Luke 2:16

They spread the word concerning what had been told them about this child, and all who heard it were amazed at what the shepherds said to them.
Luke 2:17-18

Now after Jesus was born in Bethlehem of Judea in the days of King Herod, behold, wise men from the east came to Jerusalem. Matthew 2:1

They said, "Where is he who has been born king of the Jews? For we saw his star when it rose and have come to worship him." Matthew 2:2

...the star they had seen when it rose went before them until it came to rest over the place where the child was. Matthew 2:9

And going into the house, they saw the child with Mary his mother, and they fell down and worshiped him. Matthew 2:11

Then, opening their treasures, they offered him gifts, gold and frankincense and myrrh. Matthew 2:11

For to us, a child is born, to us a son is given, and the government will be on his shoulders. And he will be called Wonderful Counselor, Mighty God, Everlasting Father, Prince of Peace. Isaiah 9:6

**Picture that glorious day Jesus was born.
Can you draw the scene of Jesus in the manger?**

Made in the USA
Las Vegas, NV
14 December 2023

82825528R00037